NM print

ALL ABOUT NEW MEXICO

100+ Interesting & Amazing Facts that everyone should know

By Bandana Ojha

Introduction

Filled with up-to-date information, fascinating & fun facts this book " All About New Mexico: Interesting & Amazing Facts that Everyone Should Know" is the best book for kids to find out more about the Land of Enchantment. This book would satisfy the children's curiosity and help them to understand why New Mexico is special—and what makes it different from other States. This book gives a story, history & explores the interesting and amazing fun facts about New Mexico. It's a fun and fascinating way for young readers to find out more New Mexico state facts and all bits of information that can touch the kid's inquisitive mind. This is a great chance for every kid to expand their knowledge about New Mexico and impress family and friends with all the discovered and never known before facts.

1. In 1540 Spanish explorer Francisco Vázquez de Coronado came to New Mexico in search of gold that were rumored to exist in the Americas. He didn't discover gold, but over the next century the Spanish colonized the land.

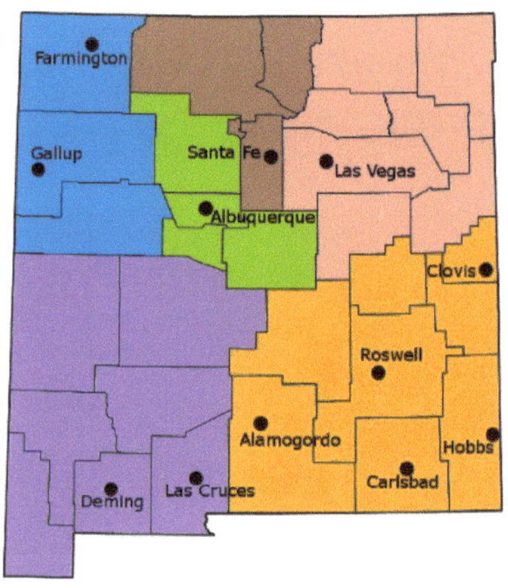

2. Then in 1821 Mexico declared its independence from Spain, and the area became part of Mexico. But after the United States won the Mexican American War in 1848, New Mexico became a U.S. territory.

3. When the Spanish set out to explore the region, they hoped to find land as valuable as what they'd found earlier in Mexico. So, they dubbed the area Nueva Mexico. (Nueva means "new" in Spanish.)

4. In 1912 it was declared the 47th state.

5. Date admitted to the Union was Saturday, January 6, 1912.

6. It is one of the Mountain States and shares the Four Corners region with Utah, Colorado, and Arizona.

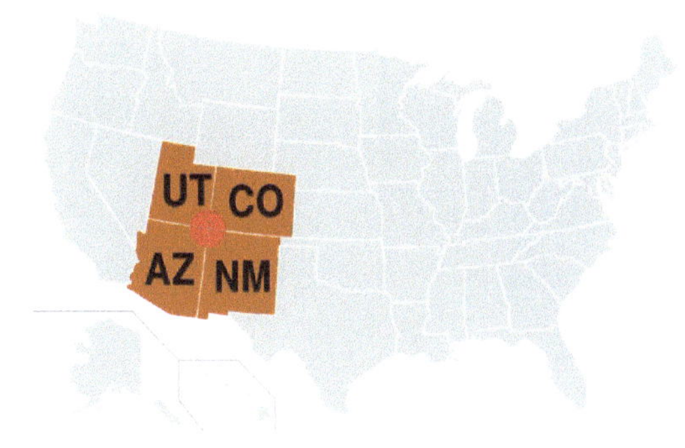

7. New Mexico is also bordered by the state of Texas to the east-southeast, Oklahoma to the northeast, and the Mexican states of Chihuahua to the south and Sonora to the southwest.

8. New Mexico is the 5th largest state (in area) in the United States (behind Alaska, Texas, California and Montana).

9. New Mexico is the 36th largest state by population.

10. New Mexico is the sixth-least densely populated of the 50 states.

11. Among U.S. states, New Mexico has the highest percentage of Hispanics, including descendants of the original Spanish colonists who have lived in the area for more than 400 years beginning in 1598.

12. It has the second-highest percentage of Native Americans as a proportion of the population after Alaska, and the fourth-highest total number of Native Americans after California, Oklahoma, and Arizona.

13. The New Mexican landscape ranges from wide, rose-colored deserts to broken mesas to high, snow-capped peaks.

14. New Mexico officially in the Mountain Time Zone.

15. State Nick Name is Land of Enchantment.

16. New Mexico Capital is Santa Fe.

17. Santa Fe was made the capital of New Mexico in 1610. It is the oldest state capital in the United States.

18. Residents of New Mexico are called New Mexican.

19. State abbreviation of New Mexico is NM.

20. State flag is the flag of New Mexico.

21. The first flag of New Mexico is one of the very few State flags ever adopted which incorporates the Stars and Stripes in its design.

22. The New Mexico state flag was officially adopted in 1925, 13 years after statehood. Winner of a design contest was an anthropologist, Dr. Harry P. Mera.

23. Dr. Harry P. Mera used a sun-symbol design from a clay pot made by an unknown woman from Zia Pueblo (Indian village) in NM.

24. There are four groups of rays with four rays in each group. This is an ancient sun symbol of a Native American people called the Zia. The Zia believed that the giver of all good gave them gifts in groups of four. These gifts are:

> The four directions – north, south, east and west.
> The four seasons – spring, summer, fall and winter.
> The day – sunrise, noon, evening and night.
> Life itself – childhood, youth, middle age and old age.

25. It is one of four U.S. state flags not to contain the color blue (the other three being Alabama, California, and Maryland).

26. The Great Seal of the State of New Mexico is the official seal of the U.S. State of New Mexico and was adopted in 1913.

27. The State motto is Crescit eundo (It grows as it goes).

28. The State flower is yucca.

29. The leaves of the Yucca can be used to make rope, baskets and sandals.

30. The State tree is pinyon.

31. The State animal is black bear.

32. The State bird is Chaparral bird.

33. The State fossil is Coelophysis.

34. The State grass is blue gramma.

35. The State amphibian is New Mexico spadefoot toad.

36. The State fish is cutthroat trout.

37. The State reptile is New Mexico
whiptail lizard.

38. The State vegetables are chili and
frijol.

39. The State gem is. Turquoise.

40. The State insect is tarantula hawk wasp.

41. The State Butterfly is Sandia hairstreak.

42. The State song is "O Fair New Mexico".

43. The State Poem is "To New Mexico".

44. The State Poem-Spanish "A Nuevo México".

45. The State Cookie is bizcochito.

46.The State historic railroad is Cumbres and Toltec Railroad.

47. The State necklace is Native American squash blossom.

48. The State colors are red and yellow.

49. Total number of counties in NM are 33.

50. Largest county by population is Bernalillo.

51. Largest county by area is Catron.

52. The State Ballad is Land of Enchantment.

53. The State tie is bolo tie.

54. The State aircraft is hot air balloon.

55. No of State parks are 31.

56. The Rio Grande is New Mexico's longest river and runs the entire length of New Mexico.

57. Albuquerque has more than 300 local hot air balloons, making it the hot air balloon capital of America with more than any other city.

58. Every October, over 500 hot air balloons and tens of thousands of balloon aficionados gather for the Albuquerque International Balloon Fiesta, which began in 1972 and has grown every year since.

59. It is the world's largest hot air balloon festival.

60. Philmont scout ranch is the Boy Scouts of America's largest National High Adventure Base. The ranch operates 35 staffed camps and 55 trail camps that range in elevation from 6,500 to 12,441 feet.

61. Hatch is known as the "Green Chile capital of the world".

62. New Mexico also has an officially designated State Question -- "Red or green?" (referring to chile preference).

63. Santa Fe is the highest capital city in the United States at 7,000 feet above sea level.

64. Santa Fe's full name is La Villa Real de la Santa Fé de San Francisco de Asís–the Royal Town of the Holy Faith of Saint Francis of Assisi.

65. The highest point in New Mexico is Wheeler Peak at 13,161 ft.

66. The lowest point in New Mexico is Red Bluff Reservoir at 2,842 feet.

67. The warmest temperature ever recorded in New Mexico was 122 °F on June 27th, 1994.

68. The coldest temperature ever recorded in New Mexico was -50 °F on February 1st, 1951.

69. New Mexico is the 23rd warmest state in the United States.

70. New Mexico has far more sheep and cattle than people. There are only about 12 people per square mile.

71. In 1607, roughly 13 years before the pilgrims landed on Plymouth Rock, Santa Fe was founded, making it the second oldest town in current day America.

72. Santa Fe's Governors Palace is the oldest government building in the country.

73. More than 500, 100-million-year-old dinosaur footprints have been identified and preserved at Clayton Lake State Park.

74. During the first 14 years of statehood, New Mexico did not have an official flag. During the San Diego World's Fair of 1915, the fair featured an exhibit hall in which all the state flags were displayed. Since New Mexico did not have an official flag, an unofficial flag was displayed, consisting of a blue field with the United States flag in the upper left corner, the words *New Mexico* and *47* in silver lettering in the center of the flag, and the state seal in the bottom right corner.

75. One out of three families in New Mexico speak Spanish at home.

76. At an elevation of 5314 feet above sea level, Albuquerque is the highest metropolitan city in the US.

77. The Bandera ice cave dates back to the 1100 B.C. This makes it one of the oldest caves in the area.

78. San Miguel Mission or San Miguel Chapel is the oldest surviving church in the United States located in Santa Fe. It is a Spanish colonial mission church built in the early 1600s. It was damaged in the Pueblo Revolt in 1680 but was resurrected again.

79. NM produced a lot of uranium in the 20th century than any other place in the US. This led to the area to be referred to as the uranium capital of the world.

80. New Mexico's capital city Santa Fe is the ending point of the 800-mile Santa Fe Trail.

81. 75% of the roads in NM are not paved This is because they are not used frequently, and the area doesn't have enough moisture to make the road disappear.

82. The four most populated cities in New Mexico are Albuquerque, Las Cruces, Rio Rancho and Santa Fe.

83. The largest city by population in New Mexico is Albuquerque.

84. The largest metropolitan area in New Mexico is the Greater Albuquerque.

85. NM is the only point in the United States where the boundaries of four states (Colorado, Utah, Arizona, and New Mexico) meet is termed as the Four Corners. Thus, one can practically stand in four states at the same time.

86. Elizabethtown, now a ghost town in Colfax County, was the first incorporated town in New Mexico.

87. Las Vegas was New Mexico's first territorial capital (for one day).

88. Public education was almost non-existent in New Mexico until the end of the 19th century. As late as 1888 there was not a single public college or high school in the entire territory.

89. The world's first Atomic Bomb was detonated on July 16, 1945 on the White Sands Testing Range near Alamogordo. The bomb was designed and manufactured in Los Alamos.

90. Native Americans from New Mexico fought for the United States in both the First and Second World Wars.

91. White Sands National Monument is a desert, not of sand, but of gleaming white gypsum crystals.

92. Smokey Bear was invented in New Mexico after the Capitan Gap fire of 1950, which burned 17,000 acres of land.

93. In NM people cannot legally dance while wearing their sombrero.

94. Located in a collapsed lave tube, the Bandera Ice Cave's temperature never rises above freezing. At the bottom of the 75-foot-deep cave, the ice floor is 20 feet thick.

95. The father of modern rocketry Massachusetts scientist Robert Goddard came to New Mexico in 1930 to test rocket-ship models. From those beginnings the aerospace industry became one of New Mexico's leading industries.

96. The Taos Pueblo, two miles north of Taos, is one of the oldest continuously occupied communities in the United States. People still live in some of its 900-year-old buildings.

97. American International Rattlesnake Museum in Albuquerque, New Mexico is home to the largest collection of different species of live rattlesnakes in the world.

98. In 1995, NM adopted an official bilingual song, "New Mexico – Mi Lindo Nuevo México".

99. In 1989, New Mexico became the first state to officially adopt the English Plus resolution, and in 2008, the first state to officially adopt a Navajo textbook for use in public schools.

100. After WWII Los Alamos and Albuquerque had many new laboratories. Hundreds of highly educated Scientists and Engineers moved in the state. New Mexico soon had a higher percentage of people with Ph.Ds. than any other state.

101. The Navajo, the Nation's largest Native American Group, have a reservation that covers 14 million Acres.

Please check this out:

Our other best-selling books for kids are-

Know about **Sharks**: 100 Amazing Fun Facts with Pictures

Know About **Whales**:100+ Amazing & Interesting Fun Facts with Pictures: " Never known Before "- Whales facts

Know About **Dinosaurs**: 100 Amazing & Interesting Fun Facts with Pictures

Know About **Kangaroos**: Amazing & Interesting Facts with Pictures

Know About **Penguins**: 100+ Amazing Penguin Facts with Pictures

Know About **Dolphins** :100 Amazing Dolphin Facts with Pictures

Know About **Elephant** :100 Amazing Dolphin Facts with Pictures

All About **New York**: 100+ Amazing Facts with Pictures

All About **New Jersey**: 100+ Amazing Facts with Pictures

All About **Massachusetts**: 100+ Amazing Facts with Pictures

All About **Florida**: 100+ Amazing Facts with Pictures

All About **California**: 100+ Amazing Facts with Pictures

All About **Arizona**: 100+ Amazing Facts with Pictures

All About **Texas**: 100+ Amazing Facts with Pictures

All About **Minnesota**: 100+ Amazing Facts with Pictures

All About **Italy**: 100+ Amazing Facts with Pictures

All About **France**: 100+ Amazing Facts with Pictures

All About **Japan:** 100 Amazing & Interesting Fun Facts

100 Amazing **Quiz Q & A About Penguin**: Never Known Before Penguin Facts

Most Popular **Animal Quiz** book for Kids: 100 amazing animal facts

Quiz Book for Kids: Science, History, Geography, Biology, Computer & Information Technology

English **Grammar** for Kids: Most Easy Way to learn English Grammar

Solar System & Space Science- Quiz for Kids: What You Know About Solar System

English **Grammar Practice** Book for elementary kids: 1000+ Practice Questions with Answers

A to Z of **English Tense**

My First **Fruits**